ONE HUNDRED
FAVOURITE
POEMS

First published in the United Kingdom in 2002 by
Frith Book Company Ltd

Text and Design copyright © Frith Book Company Ltd
Photographs copyright © The Francis Frith Collection

The Frith photographs and the Frith logo are reproduced under licence from
Heritage Photographic Resources Ltd, the owners of the Frith archive and
trademarks

British Library Cataloguing in Publication Data
One Hundred Favourite Poems
ISBN 1-85937-540-5

Frith Book Company Ltd
Frith's Barn, Teffont,
Salisbury, Wiltshire SP3 5QP
Tel: +44 (0) 1722 716 376
Email: info@francisfrith.co.uk
www.francisfrith.co.uk

Printed and bound in Spain

CONTENTS

1 *The Lake Isle of Innisfree*

I WILL arise and go now, and go to Innisfree,
And a small cabin build there, of clay and wattles made:
Nine bean-rows will I have there, a hive for the honey-bee,
And live alone in the bee-loud glade.

And I shall have some peace there, for peace comes
   dropping slow,
Dropping from the veils of the morning to where the
   cricket sings;
There midnight's all a glimmer, and noon a purple glow,
And evening full of the linnet's wings.

I will arise and go now, for always night and day
I hear lake water lapping with low sounds by the shore;
While I stand on the roadway, or on the pavements grey,
I hear it in the deep heart's core.

W B YEATS (1865-1939)

2 *Afternoon on a Hill*

I WILL be the gladdest thing
  Under the sun!
I will touch a hundred flowers
  And not pick one.
I will look at cliffs and clouds
  With quiet eyes,
Watch the wind bow down the grass,
  And the grass rise.
And when lights begin to show
  Up from the town,
I will mark which must be mine,
  And then start down!

EDNA ST VINCENT MILLAY (1892-1950)

3 *Pippa's Song (from Pippa Passes)*

THE year's at the spring,
  And day's at the morn;
    Morning's at seven;
      The hill-side's dew-pearl'd;
The lark's on the wing;
  The snail's on the thorn:
    God's in His heaven—
      All's right with the world!

ROBERT BROWNING (1812-1889)

4 *The Character of a Happy Life*

HOW happy is he born or taught
  That serveth not another's will;
Whose armour is his honest thought,
  And simple truth his utmost skill!
Whose passions not his masters are;
  Whose soul is still prepared for death,
Untied unto the world by care
  Of princes' grace or vulgar breath;
Who envies none that chance doth raise,
  Nor vice; who never understood
How deepest wounds are given by praise;
  Nor rules of state but rules of good;
Who hath his life from rumours freed;
  Whose conscience is his strong retreat;
Whose state can neither flatterers feed,
  Nor ruin make accusers great;
Who God doth late and early pray
  More of His grace than gifts to lend;
And entertains the harmless day
  With a well-chosen book or friend;
—This man is freed from servile bands
  Of hope to rise or fear to fall:
Lord of himself, though not of lands,
  And having nothing, yet hath all.

SIR HENRY WOTTON (1568-1639)

5 *The Argument of His Book*

I SING of brooks, of blossoms, birds and bowers;
Of April, May, of June, and July flowers.
I sing of May-poles, hock-carts, wassails, wakes,
Of bridegrooms, brides and of their bridal-cakes.
I write of youth, of love, and have access
By these to sing of cleanly wantonness.
I sing of dews, of rains, and piece by piece,
Of balm, of oil, of spice, of ambergris.
I sing of times trans-shifting, and I write
How roses first came red, and lilies white.
I write of groves, of twilights, and I sing
The court of Mab, and of the Fairy King.
I write of Hell; I sing (and ever shall)
Of Heaven, and hope to have it after all.

ROBERT HERRICK (1591-1674)

6 *Ye Flowery Banks*

YE FLOWERY banks o' bonnie Doon,
  How can ye bloom sae fair!
How can ye chant, ye little birds,
  And I sae fu' o' care!
Thou'll break my heart, thou bonnie bird,
  That sings upon the bough;
Thou minds me o' the happy days
  When my fause Luve was true.
Thou'll break my heart, thou bonnie bird
  That sings beside thy mate;
For sae I sat, and sae I sang,
  And wist na o' my fate.
Aft hae I roved by bonnie Doon
  To see the woodbine twine;
And ilka bird sang o' its luve,
  And sae did I o' mine.
Wi lightsome heart I pu'd a rose,
  Frae aff its thorny tree;
And my fause luver staw the rose,
  But left the thorn wi'me.

ROBERT BURNS (1759-1796)

7 *from As You Like It*

UNDER the greenwood tree
Who loves to lie with me,
And turn his merry note
Unto the sweet bird's throat,
Come hither, come hither, come hither!
Here shall he see
No enemy
But winter and rough weather.

Who doth ambition shun
And loves to live i' the sun,
Seeking the food he eats,
And pleased with what he gets,
Come hither, come hither, come hither!
Here shall he see
No enemy
But winter and rough weather.

WILLIAM SHAKESPEARE (1564-1616)

8 *To the Virgins, to Make Much of Time*

GATHER ye rosebuds while ye may,
  Old Time is still a-flying;
And this same flower that smiles today,
  Tomorrow will be dying.

The glorious lamp of heaven, the Sun,
  The higher he's a-getting,
The sooner will his race be run,
  And nearer he's to setting.

That age is best which is the first,
  When youth and blood are warmer,
But being spent, the worse, and worst
  Times still succeed the former.

Then be not coy, but use your time,
  And while ye may, go marry:
For having lost but once your prime,
  You may forever tarry.

ROBERT HERRICK (1591-1674)

9 *Leisure*

WHAT is this life if, full of care,
We have no time to stand and stare.

No time to stand beneath the boughs
And stare as long as sheep or cows.

No time to see, when woods we pass,
Where squirrels hide their nuts in grass.

No time to see, in broad daylight,
Streams full of stars like skies at night.

No time to turn at Beauty's glance,
And watch her feet, how they can dance.

No time to wait till her mouth can
Enrich that smile her eyes began.

A poor life this if, full of care,
We have no time to stand and stare.

W H DAVIES (1871-1940)

10 *from I Remember, I Remember*

I REMEMBER, I remember,
The house where I was born,
The little window where the sun
Came peeping in at morn;
He never came a wink too soon,
Nor brought too long a day,
But now, I often wish the night
Had borne my breath away! …

I remember, I remember
The fir trees dark and high;
I used to think their slender tops
Were close against the sky:
It was a childish ignorance,
But now 'tis little joy
To know I'm farther off from Heaven
Than when I was a boy.

THOMAS HOOD (1799-1845)

11 *Child*

YOUR clear eye is the one absolutely beautiful thing.
I want to fill it with colour and ducks,
The zoo of the new

Whose names you meditate—
April snowdrop, Indian pipe,
Little

Stalk without wrinkle,
Pool in which images
Should be grand and classical

Not this troublous
Wringing of hands, this dark
Ceiling without a star.

SYLVIA PLATH (1932-1963)

12 *Morning Song*

LOVE set you going like a fat gold watch.
The midwife slapped your footsoles, and your bald cry
Took its place among the elements.

Our voices echo, magnifying your arrival. New statue.
In a drafty museum, your nakedness
Shadows our safety. We stand round blankly as walls.

I'm no more your mother
Than the cloud that distills a mirror to reflect its own slow
Effacement at the wind's hand.

All night your moth-breath
Flickers among the flat pink roses. I wake to listen:
A far sea moves in my ear.

One cry, and I stumble from bed, cow-heavy and floral
In my Victorian nightgown.
Your mouth opens clean as a cat's. The window square

Whitens and swallows its dull stars. And now you try
Your handful of notes;
The clear vowels rise like balloons.

SYLVIA PLATH (1932-1963)

13 After-Thought, Sonnets from the River Duddon

I THOUGHT of Thee, my partner and my guide,
As being past away.—Vain sympathies!
For, backward, Duddon! as I cast my eyes,
I see what was, and is, and will abide;
Still glides the stream, and shall for ever glide;
The Form remains, the Function never dies;
While we, the brave, the mighty, and the wise,
We Men, who in our morn of youth defied
The elements, must vanish;—be it so!
Enough, if something from our hands have power
To live, and act, and serve the future hour;
And if, as toward the silent tomb we go,
Through love, through hope, and faith's transcendent dower,
We feel that we are greater than we know.

WILLIAM WORDSWORTH (1770-1850)

14 *from The Brook*

... I WIND about, and in and out,
  With here a blossom sailing,
And here and there a lusty trout,
  And here and there a grayling,

And here and there a foamy flake
  Upon me, as I travel
With many a silvery waterbreak
  Above the golden gravel ...

I slip, I slide, I gloom, I glance,
  Among my skimming swallows;
I make the netted sunbeam dance
  Against my sandy shallows.

I murmur under moon and stars
  In brambly wildernesses;
I linger by my shingly bars;
  I loiter round my cresses;

And out again I curve and flow
  To join the brimming river,
For men may come and men may go,
  But I go on for ever.

ALFRED, LORD TENNYSON (1809-1892)

15 *from The Retreat*

HAPPY those early days, when I
Shin'd in my angel-infancy!
Before I understood this place
Appointed for my second race,
Or taught my soul to fancy ought
But a white, celestial thought;
When yet I had not walk'd above
A mile or two from my first love,
And looking back, at that short space
Could see a glimpse of His bright face;
When on some gilded cloud, or flow'r,
My gazing soul would dwell an hour,
And in those weaker glories spy
Some shadows of eternity …

O how I long to travel back,
And tread again that ancient track!
That I might once more reach that plain,
Where first I left my glorious train;
From whence th' enlighten'd spirit sees
That shady City of palm-trees.
But ah! my soul with too much stay
Is drunk, and staggers in the way!
Some men a forward motion love,
But I by backward steps would move;
And when this dust falls to the urn,
In that state I came, return.

HENRY VAUGHAN (1622-1695)

16 *from Auguries of Innocence*

TO SEE a World in a Grain of Sand
And a Heaven in a Wild Flower,
Hold Infinity in the palm of your hand
And Eternity in an hour.

A Robin Redbreast in a Cage
Puts all Heaven in a Rage.
A dove house fill'd with Doves & Pigeons
Shudders Hell thro' all its regions.
A dog starv'd at his Master's Gate
Predicts the ruin of the State.
A Horse misus'd upon the Road
Calls to Heaven for Human blood.
Each outcry of the hunted Hare
A fibre from the Brain does tear.
A Skylark wounded in the wing,
A Cherubim does cease to sing ...

WILLIAM BLAKE (1757-1827)

17 *from If . . .*

IF YOU can keep your head when all about you
  Are losing theirs and blaming it on you,
If you can trust yourself when all men doubt you,
  But make allowance for their doubting too;
If you can wait and not be tired by waiting,
  Or being lied about, don't deal in lies,
Or being hated, don't give way to hating,
  And yet don't look too good, nor talk too wise: ...

If you can make one heap of all your winnings
  And risk it on one turn of pitch-and-toss,
And lose, and start again at your beginnings
  And never breathe a word about your loss;
If you can force your heart and nerve and sinew
  To serve your turn long after they are gone,
And so hold on when there is nothing in you
  Except the Will which says to them: "Hold on!"

If you can talk with crowds and keep your virtue,
  Or walk with Kings—nor lose the common touch,
If neither foes nor loving friends can hurt you,
  If all men count with you, but none too much;
If you can fill the unforgiving minute
  With sixty seconds' worth of distance run,
Yours is the Earth and everything that's in it,
  And—which is more—you'll be a man, my son!

RUDYARD KIPLING (1865-1936)

18 *Young And Old*

WHEN all the world is young, lad,
  And all the trees are green;
And every goose a swan, lad,
  And every lass a queen;
Then hey for boot and horse, lad,
  And round the world away;
Young blood must have its course, lad,
  And every dog his day.

When all the world is old, lad,
  And all the trees are brown;
And all the sport is stale, lad,
  And all the wheels run down;
Creep home, and take your place there,
  The spent and maimed among:
God grant you find one face there,
  You loved when all was young.

CHARLES KINGSLEY (1819-1875)

19 *The Three Fishers*

THREE fishers went sailing away to the west,
  Away to the west as the sun went down;
Each thought on the woman who loved him the best,
  And the children stood watching them out of the town;
  For men must work, and women must weep,
  And there's little to earn, and many to keep,
    Though the harbour bar be moaning.

Three wives sat up in the lighthouse tower,
  And they trimmed the lamps as the sun went down;
They looked at the squall, and they looked at the shower,
  And the night-rack came rolling up ragged and brown.
  But men must work, and women must weep,
  Though storms be sudden, and waters deep,
    And the harbour bar be moaning.

Three corpses lay out on the shining sands
  In the morning gleam as the tide went down,
And the women are weeping and wringing their hands
  For those who will never come home to the town;
  For men must work, and women must weep,
  And the sooner it's over, the sooner to sleep;
    And good-bye to the bar and its moaning.

CHARLES KINGSLEY (1819-1875)

20 *Crossing the Bar*

SUNSET and evening star,
   And one clear call for me!
And may there be no moaning of the bar,
   When I put out to sea,

But such a tide as moving seems asleep,
   Too full for sound and foam,
When that which drew from out the boundless deep
   Turns again home.

Twilight and evening bell,
   And after that the dark!
And may there be no sadness of farewell,
   When I embark;

For tho' from out our bourne of Time and Place
   The flood may bear me far,
I hope to see my Pilot face to face
   When I have crossed the bar.

ALFRED, LORD TENNYSON (1809-1892)

21 *from Dover Beach*

THE sea is calm tonight.
The tide is full, the moon lies fair
Upon the straits; —on the French coast the light
Gleams and is gone; the cliffs of England stand,
Glimmering and vast, out in the tranquil bay.
Come to the window, sweet is the night air!
Only, from the long line of spray
Where the sea meets the moon-blanched land,
Listen! you hear the grating roar
Of pebbles which the waves draw back, and fling,
At their return, up the high strand,
Begin, and cease, and then again begin,
With tremulous cadence slow, and bring
The eternal note of sadness in …

Ah, love, let us be true
To one another! for the world, which seems
To lie before us like a land of dreams,
So various, so beautiful, so new,
Hath really neither joy, nor love, nor light,
Nor certitude, nor peace, nor help for pain;
And we are here as on a darkling plain
Swept with confused alarms of struggle and flight,
Where ignorant armies clash by night.

MATTHEW ARNOLD (1822-1888)

22 *Farewell to Arms: To Queen Elizabeth*

HIS golden locks time hath to silver turned;
    O time too swift, O swiftness never ceasing!
His youth 'gainst time and age hath ever spurned,
    But spurned in vain; youth waneth by increasing:
Beauty, strength, youth, are flowers but fading seen;
Duty, faith, love, are roots, and ever green.

His helmet now shall make a hive for bees;
    And, lovers' sonnets turned to holy psalms,
A man-at-arms must now serve on his knees,
    And feed on prayers, which are age's alms:
But though from court to cottage he depart,
His saint is sure of his unspotted heart.

And when he saddest sits in homely cell,
    He'll teach his swains this carol for a song:
'Blest be the hearts that wish my sovereign well,
    Curst be the souls that think her any wrong'.
Goddess, allow this aged man his right,
To be your beadsman now, that was your knight.

GEORGE PEELE (?1558-1596)

23 *The Send-Off*

DOWN the close, darkening lanes they sang their way
To the siding-shed,
And lined the train with faces grimly gay.

Their breasts were stuck all white with wreath and
spray
As men's are, dead.

Dull porters watched them, and a casual tramp
Stood staring hard,
Sorry to miss them from the upland camp.
Then, unmoved, signals nodded, and a lamp
Winked to the guard.

So secretly, like wrongs hushed-up, they went.
They were not ours:
We never heard to which front these were sent.

Nor there if they yet mock what women meant
Who gave them flowers.

Shall they return to beatings of great bells
In wild train-loads?
A few, a few, too few for drums and yells,
May creep back, silent, to village wells
Up half-known roads.

WILFRED OWEN (1893-1918)

24 *from The Charge of the Light Brigade 1854*

HALF a league, half a league,
　　Half a league onward,
All in the valley of Death
　　Rode the six hundred.
'Forward, the Light Brigade!
Charge for the guns!' he said;
Into the valley of Death
　　Rode the six hundred.

'Forward, the Light Brigade!'
Was there a man dismay'd?
Not tho' the soldier knew
　　Some one had blunder'd:
Their's not to make reply,
Their's not to reason why,
Their's but to do and die …

Cannon to right of them,
Cannon to left of them,
Cannon in front of them
　　Volley'd and thunder'd;
Storm'd at with shot and shell,
Boldly they rode and well,
Into the jaws of Death,
Into the mouth of Hell
　　Rode the six hundred …

ALFRED, LORD TENNYSON (1809-1892)

25 *The Soldier*

IF I should die, think only this of me:
　　That there's some corner of a foreign field
That is for ever England. There shall be
　　In that rich earth a richer dust concealed;
A dust whom England bore, shaped, made aware,
　　Gave, once her flowers to love, her ways to roam,
A body of England's, breathing English air,
　　Washed by the rivers, blest by suns of home.

And think, this heart, all evil shed away,
　　A pulse in the eternal mind, no less
　　　　Gives somewhere back the thoughts by England given;
Her sights and sounds; dreams happy as her day;
　　And laughter, learnt of friends; and gentleness,
　　　　In hearts at peace, under an English heaven.

RUPERT BROOKE (1887-1915)

26 *So, We'll Go No More a-Roving*

SO, WE'LL go no more a-roving
  So late into the night,
Though the heart be still as loving,
  And the moon be still as bright.

For the sword outwears its sheath,
  And the soul wears out the breast,
And the heart must pause to breathe,
  And love itself have rest.

Though the night was made for loving,
  And the day returns too soon,
Yet we'll go no more a-roving
  By the light of the moon.

GEORGE GORDON, LORD BYRON (1788-1824)

27 *from Auld Lang Syne*

SHOULD auld acquaintance be forgot,
    And never brought to mind?
Should auld acquaintance be forgot,
    And auld lang syne!

    For auld lang syne, my dear,
        For auld lang syne,
   We'll tak a cup o' kindness yet,
        For auld lang syne.

We twa hae run about the braes,
    And pou'd the gowans fine;
But we've wander'd mony a weary foot,
    Sin' auld lang syne.

We twa hae paidl'd i' the burn,
    Frae morning sun till dine;
But seas between us braid hae roar'd
    Sin' auld lang syne ...

And surely ye'll be your pint stowp,
    And surely I'll be mine;
And we'll tak a cup o' kindness yet,
    For auld lang syne.

ROBERT BURNS (1759-1796)

28 *The Road Not Taken*

TWO roads diverged in a yellow wood,
And sorry I could not travel both
And be one traveller, long I stood
And looked down one as far as I could
To where it bent in the undergrowth;

Then took the other, as just as fair,
And having perhaps the better claim,
Because it was grassy and wanted wear;
Though as for that the passing there
Had worn them really about the same,

And both that morning equally lay
In leaves no step had trodden black.
Oh, I kept the first for another day!
Yet knowing how way leads on to way,
I doubted if I should ever come back.

I shall be telling this with a sigh
Somewhere ages and ages hence:
Two roads diverged in a wood, and I—
I took the one less travelled by,
And that has made all the difference.

ROBERT FROST (1874-1963)

29 *Hope is a thing with feathers*

'HOPE' is the thing with feathers—
That perches in the soul—
And sings the tune without the words—
And never stops—at all—

And sweetest—in the Gale—is heard—
And sore must be the storm—
That could abash the little Bird
That keeps so many warm—

I've heard it in the chillest land—
And on the strangest Sea—
Yet, never, in Extremity
It asked a crumb—of Me.

EMILY DICKINSON (1830-1886)

30 *from To Althea from Prison*

… STONE walls do not a prison make,
    Nor iron bars a cage;
Minds innocent and quiet take
    That for an hermitage:
If I have freedom in my love,
    And in my soul am free,
Angels alone, that soar above,
    Enjoy such liberty.

RICHARD LOVELACE (1618-1658)

31 *from Macbeth*

MACBETH: To-morrow, and to-morrow, and to-morrow,
Creeps in this petty pace from day to day,
To the last syllable of recorded time;
And all our yesterdays have lighted fools
The way to dusty death. Out, out, brief candle!
Life's but a walking shadow, a poor player,
That struts and frets his hour upon the stage,
And then is heard no more; it is a tale
Told by an idiot, full of sound and fury,
Signifying nothing.

WILLIAM SHAKESPEARE (1564-1616)

32 *Even Such is Time*

EVEN such is time, which takes in trust
Our youth, our joys, and all we have,
And pays us but with age and dust;
Who, in the dark and silent grave,
When we have wandered all our ways,
Shuts up the story of our days,
And from which earth and grave and dust,
The Lord shall raise me up, I trust.

SIR WALTER RALEIGH (?1552–1618)

33 *Childhood*

I USED to think that grown-up people chose
To have stiff backs and wrinkles round their nose,
And veins like small fat snakes on either hand,
On purpose to be grand.
Till through the banisters I watched one day
My great-aunt Etty's friend who was going away,
And how her onyx beads had come unstrung.
I saw her grope to find them as they rolled;
And then I knew that she was helplessly old,
As I was helplessly young.

FRANCES CORNFORD (1886-1960)

34 *from Cymbeline*

FEAR no more the heat o' the sun,
    Nor the furious winter's rages;
Thou thy worldly task hast done,
    Home art gone, and ta'en thy wages;
Golden lads and girls all must,
As chimney-sweepers, come to dust.

Fear no more the frown o' the great,
    Thou art past the tyrant's stroke;
Care no more to clothe and eat;
    To thee the reed is as the oak:
The sceptre, learning, physic, must
All follow this, and come to dust.

Fear no more the lightning-flash
    Nor the all-dreaded thunder-stone;
Fear not slander, censure rash;
    Thou hast finish'd joy and moan:
All lovers young, all lovers must
Consign to thee, and come to dust ...

WILLIAM SHAKESPEARE (1564-1616)

35 *Winter Ride*

WHO shall declare the joy of the running!
    Who shall tell of the pleasures of flight!
Springing and spurning the tufts of wild heather,
    Sweeping, wide-winged, through the blue dome of light.
Everything mortal has moments immortal,
    Swift and God-gifted, immeasurably bright.
So with the stretch of the white road before me,
    Shining snowcrystals rainbowed by the sun,
Fields that are white, stained with long, cool, blue shadows,
    Strong with the strength of my horse as we run.
Joy in the touch of the wind and the sunlight!
    Joy! With the vigorous earth I am one.

AMY LOWELL (1874-1925)

EVERY branch big with it,
     Bent every twig with it;
Every fork like a white web-foot;
Every street and pavement mute;
Some flakes have lost their way, and grope back upward, when
Meeting those meandering down they turn and descend again.
     The palings are glued together like a wall,
     And there is no waft of wind with the fleecy fall.

     A sparrow enters the tree,
     Whereon immediately
A snow-lump thrice his own slight size
Descends on him and showers his head and eyes,
     And overturns him,
     And near inurns him,
And lights on a nether twig, when its brush
Starts off a volley of other lodging lumps with a rush.

     The steps are a blanched slope,
     Up which, with feeble hope,
A black cat comes, wide-eyed and thin;
     And we take him in.

THOMAS HARDY (1840-1928)

37 *from In Memoriam*

RING out, wild bells, to the wild sky,
    The flying cloud, the frosty light:
    The year is dying in the night;
Ring out, wild bells, and let him die.

Ring out the old, ring in the new,
    Ring, happy bells, across the snow:
    The year is going, let him go;
Ring out the false, ring in the true.

Ring out the grief that saps the mind,
    For those that here we see no more;
    Ring out the feud of rich and poor,
Ring in redress to all mankind …

Ring out the want, the care, the sin,
    The faithless coldness of the times;
    Ring out, ring out my mournful rhymes,
But ring the fuller minstrel in.

Ring out false pride in place and blood,
    The civic slander and the spite;
    Ring in the love of truth and right,
Ring in the common love of good …

ALFRED, LORD TENNYSON (1809-1892)

38 *from Written in March*

THE cock is crowing,
The stream is flowing,
The small birds twitter,
The lake doth glitter,
The green field sleeps in the sun ...

Like an army defeated
The snow hath retreated,
And now doth fare ill
On the top of the bare hill;
The plowboy is whooping–anon–anon:

There's joy in the mountains;
There's life in the fountains;
Small clouds are sailing,
Blue sky prevailing;
The rain is over and gone!

WILLIAM WORDSWORTH (1770-1850)

39 *from The Village Blacksmith*

UNDER a spreading chestnut-tree
 The village smithy stands;
The smith, a mighty man is he,
 With large and sinewy hands;
And the muscles of his brawny arms
 Are strong as iron bands.
His hair is crisp, and black, and long,
 His face is like the tan;
His brow is wet with honest sweat,
 He earns whate'er he can,
And looks the whole world in the face,
 For he owes not any man.
Week in, week out, from morn till night,
 You can hear his bellows blow;
You can hear him swing his heavy sledge,
 With measured beat and slow,
Like a sexton ringing the village bell,
 When the evening sun is low.
And children coming home from school
 Look in at the open door;
They love to see the flaming forge,
 And hear the bellows roar,
And catch the burning sparks that fly
 Like chaff from a threshing-floor.

HENRY WADSWORTH LONGFELLOW (1807–1882)

40 *Little Trotty Wagtail*

LITTLE Trotty Wagtail, he went in the rain,
And tittering, tottering sideways he ne'er got straight again.
He stooped to get a worm, and look'd up to get a fly,
And then he flew away ere his feathers they were dry.

Little Trotty Wagtail, he waddled in the mud,
And left his little footmarks, trample where he would.
He waddled in the water-pudge and waggle went his tail,
And he chirrup up his wings to dry upon the garden rail.

Little Trotty Wagtail, you nimble all about,
And in the dimpling water-pudge you waddle in and out;
Your home is nigh at hand, and in the warm pig stye,
So, little Master Wagtail, I'll bid you a goodbye.

JOHN CLARE (1793-1864)

41 *Weathers*

THIS is the weather the cuckoo likes,
And so do I;
When showers betumble the chestnut spikes,
And nestlings fly;
And the little brown nightingale bills his best,
And they sit outside at 'The Traveller's Rest,'
And maids come forth sprig-muslin drest,
And citizens dream of the south and west,
And so do I.

This is the weather the shepherd shuns,
And so do I;
When beeches drip in browns and duns,
And thresh and ply;
And hill-hid tides throb, throe on throe,
And meadow rivulets overflow,
And drops on gate bars hang in a row,
And rooks in families homeward go,
And so do I.

THOMAS HARDY (1840-1928)

42 *from Baby Tortoise*

YOU know what it is to be born alone,
Baby tortoise!

The first day to heave your feet little by little from
   the shell,
Not yet awake,
And remain lapsed on earth,
Not quite alive.

A tiny, fragile, half-animate bean.

To open your tiny beak-mouth, that looks as if it would
   never open
Like some iron door;
To lift the upper hawk-beak from the lower base
And reach your skinny neck
And take your first bite at some dim bit of herbage,
Alone, small insect,
Tiny bright-eye,
Slow one …

D H LAWRENCE (1885-1930)

43 *from The Elephant is Slow to Mate*

THE elephant, the huge old beast,
    is slow to mate;
he finds a female, they show no haste
    they wait

for the sympathy in their vast shy hearts
    slowly, slowly to rouse
as they loiter along the river-beds
    and drink and browse

and dash in panic through the brake
    of forest with the herd,
and sleep in massive silence, and wake
    together, without a word.

So slowly the great hot elephant hearts
    grow full of desire,
and the great beasts mate in secret at last,
    hiding their fire.

Oldest they are and the wisest of beasts
    so they know at last
how to wait for the loneliest of feasts
    for the full repast ...

D H LAWRENCE (1885-1930)

44 *from To a Skylark*

HAIL to thee, blithe Spirit!
    Bird thou never wert—
That from Heaven or near it
    Pourest thy full heart
In profuse strains of unpremeditated art.

Higher still and higher
    From the earth thou springest,
Like a cloud of fire;
    The blue deep thou wingest,
And singing still dost soar, and soaring ever singest.

In the golden lightning
    Of the sunken sun,
O'er which clouds are bright'ning,
    Thou dost float and run,
Like an unbodied joy whose race is just begun …

Teach me half the gladness
    That thy brain must know;
Such harmonious madness
    From my lips would flow,
The world should listen then, as I am listening now!

PERCY BYSSHE SHELLEY (1792-1822)

45 *from The Daffodils*

I WANDERED lonely as a cloud
   That floats on high o'er vales and hills,
When all at once I saw a crowd,
   A host, of golden daffodils,
Beside the lake, beneath the trees,
Fluttering and dancing in the breeze.

Continuous as the stars that shine
   And twinkle on the Milky Way,
They stretched in never-ending line
   Along the margin of a bay:
Ten thousand saw I at a glance,
Tossing their heads in sprightly dance …

WILLIAM WORDSWORTH (1770-1850)

46 *from Endymion*

A THING of beauty is a joy for ever:
Its loveliness increases; it will never
Pass into nothingness; but still will keep
A bower quiet for us, and a sleep
Full of sweet dreams, and health, and quiet breathing.
Therefore, on every morrow, are we wreathing
A flowery band to bind us to the earth,
Spite of despondence, of the inhuman dearth
Of noble natures, of the gloomy days,
Of all the unhealthy and o'er-darkn'd ways
Made for our searching: yes, in spite of all,
Some shape of beauty moves away the pall
From our dark spirits. Such the sun, the moon,
Trees old, and young, sprouting a shady boon
For simple sheep; and such are daffodils
With the green world they live in; and clear rills
That for themselves a cooling covert make
'Gainst the hot season; the mid forest brake,
Rich with a sprinkling of fair musk-rose blooms:
And such too is the grandeur of the dooms
We have imagined for the mighty dead;
All lovely tales that we have heard or read:
An endless fountain of immortal drink,
Pouring unto us from the heaven's brink …

JOHN KEATS (1795-1821)

47 *The Vixen*

AMONG the taller wood with ivy hung,
The old fox plays and dances round her young.
She snuffs and barks if any passes by
And swings her tail and turns prepared to fly.
The horseman hurries by, she bolts to see,
And turns agen, from danger never free.
If any stands she runs among the poles
And barks and snaps and drives them in the holes.
The shepherd sees them and the boy goes by
And gets a stick and progs the hole to try.
They get all still and lie in safety sure,
And out again when everything's secure,
And start and snap at blackbirds bouncing by
To fight and catch the great white butterfly.

JOHN CLARE (1793-1864)

48 *The Baby*

WHERE did you come from, baby dear?
  Out of the everywhere into here.
Where did you get those eyes so blue?
  Out of the sky as I came through.
What makes the light in them sparkle and spin?
  Some of the starry spikes left in.
Where did you get that little tear?
  I found it waiting when I got here.
What makes your forehead so smooth and high?
  A soft hand stroked it as I went by.
What makes your cheek like a warm white rose?
  I saw something better than any one knows.
Whence that three-cornered smile of bliss?
  Three angels gave me at once a kiss.
Where did you get this pearly ear?
  God spoke, and it came out to hear.
Where did you get those arms and hands?
  Love made itself into bonds and bands.
Feet, whence did you come, you darling things?
  From the same box as the cherub's wings.
How did they all just come to be you?
  God thought about me, and so I grew.
But how did you come to us, you dear?
  God thought about you, and so I am here.

GEORGE MACDONALD (1824-1905)

49 *The Pike*

IN THE brown water,
Thick and silver-sheened in the sunshine,
Liquid and cool in the shade of the reeds,
A pike dozed.
Lost among the shadows of stems
He lay unnoticed.
Suddenly he flicked his tail,
And a green-and-copper brightness
Ran under the water.
Out from under the reeds
Came the olive-green light,
And orange flashed up
Through the sun-thickened water.
So the fish passed across the pool,
Green and copper,
A darkness and a gleam,
And the blurred reflections of the willows on the
    opposite bank
Received it.

AMY LOWELL (1874-1925)

50 *The Maldive Shark*

ABOUT the Shark, phlegmatical one,
Pale sot of the Maldive sea,
The sleek little pilot-fish, azure and slim,
How alert in attendance be.
From his saw-pit of mouth, from his charnel of maw
They have nothing of harm to dread,
But liquidly glide on his ghastly flank
Or before his Gorgonian head;
Or lurk in the port of serrated teeth
In white triple tiers of glittering gates,
And there find a haven when peril's abroad,
An asylum in jaws of the Fates!
They are friends; and friendly they guide him to prey,
Yet never partake of the treat—
Eyes and brains to the dotard lethargic and dull,
Pale ravener of horrible meat.

HERMAN MELVILLE (1819-1891)

51 *The Solitary Reaper*

BEHOLD her, single in the field,
  Yon solitary Highland Lass!
Reaping and singing by herself;
  Stop here, or gently pass!
Alone she cuts and binds the grain,
And sings a melancholy strain;
O listen! for the vale profound
Is overflowing with the sound.

No nightingale did ever chaunt
  More welcome notes to weary bands
Of travellers in some shady haunt,
  Among Arabian sands:
A voice so thrilling ne'er was heard
In spring-time from the cuckoo-bird,
Breaking the silence of the seas
Among the farthest Hebrides.

Will no one tell me what she sings?—
  Perhaps the plaintive numbers flow
For old, unhappy, far-off things,
  And battles long ago:
Or is it some more humble lay,
Familiar matter of to-day?
Some natural sorrow, loss, or pain,
That has been, and may be again?

Whate'er the theme, the maiden sang
    As if her song could have no ending;
I saw her singing at her work,
    And o'er the sickle bending;—
I listened, motionless and still;
And, as I mounted up the hill,
The music in my heart I bore,
Long after it was heard no more.

WILLIAM WORDSWORTH (1770-1850)

52 *from Ode to a Nightingale*

MY HEART aches, and a drowsy numbness pains
    My sense, as though of hemlock I had drunk,
Or emptied some dull opiate to the drains
    One minute past, and Lethe-wards had sunk:
'Tis not through envy of thy happy lot,
    But being too happy in thine happiness,
        That thou, light-winged Dryad of the trees,
            In some melodious plot
    Of beechen green, and shadows numberless,
        Singest of summer in full-throated ease.

O for a draught of vintage! that hath been
    Cool'd a long age in the deep-delved earth,
Tasting of Flora and the country green,
    Dance, and Provençal song, and sunburnt mirth! …

JOHN KEATS (1795-1821)

53 *from The Tempest*

WHERE the bee sucks, there suck I,
In a cowslip's bell I lie,
There I couch when owls do cry,
On the bat's back I do fly
After summer merrily.
    Merrily, merrily, shall I live now
    Under the blossom that hangs on the bough.

WILLIAM SHAKESPEARE (1564–1616)

54 *East Anglian Bathe*

OH WHEN the early morning at the seaside
   Took us with hurrying steps from Horsey Mere
To see the whistling bent-grass on the leeside
   And then the tumbled breaker-line appear,
On high, the clouds with mighty adumbration
   Sailed over us to seaward fast and clear
And jellyfish in quivering isolation
   Lay silted in the dry sand of the breeze
And we, along the table-land of beach blown
   Went gooseflesh from our shoulders to our knees
And ran to catch the football, each to each thrown,
   In the soft and swirling music of the seas.

There splashed about our ankles as we waded
   Those intersecting wavelets morning-cold,
And sudden dark a patch of sea was shaded,
   And sudden light, another patch would hold
The warmth of whirling atoms in a sun-shot
   And underwater sandstorm green and gold.
So in we dived and louder than a gunshot
   Sea-water broke in fountains down the ear.
How cold the bathe, how chattering cold the drying,
   How welcoming the inland reeds appear,
The wood-smoke and the breakfast and the frying,
   And your warm freshwater ripples, Horsey Mere.

SIR JOHN BETJEMAN (1906-1984)

55 *from The Ancient Mariner*

… DOWN dropt the breeze, the sails dropt down,
'Twas sad as sad could be;
And we did speak only to break
The silence of the sea!

All in a hot and copper sky,
The bloody Sun, at noon,
Right up above the mast did stand,
No bigger than the Moon.

Day after day, day after day,
We stuck, nor breath nor motion;
As idle as a painted ship
Upon a painted ocean.

Water, water, every where,
And all the boards did shrink;
Water, water, every where,
Nor any drop to drink …

About, about, in reel and rout
The death-fires danced at night;
The water, like a witch's oils,
Burnt green, and blue and white …

SAMUEL TAYLOR COLERIDGE (1772-1834)

56 *The Poplar-Field*

THE poplars are felled, farewell to the shade
And the whispering sound of the cool colonnade!
The winds play no longer, and sing in the leaves,
Nor Ouse on his bosom their image receives.

Twelve years have elapsed since I first took a view
Of my favourite field, and the bank where they grew,
And now in the grass behold they are laid,
And the tree is my seat that once lent me a shade.

The blackbird has fled to another retreat
Where the hazels afford him a screen from the heat,
And the scene where his melody charmed me before
Resounds with his sweet-flowing ditty no more.

My fugitive years are all hasting away,
And I must ere long lie as lowly as they,
With a turf on my breast, and a stone at my head,
Ere another such grove shall arise in its stead.

'Tis a sight to engage me, if anything can,
To muse on the perishing pleasures of man;
Though his life be a dream, his enjoyments, I see,
Have a being less durable even than he.

WILLIAM COWPER (1731-1800)

57 *from Woodman, Spare That Tree!*

WOODMAN, spare that tree!
Touch not a single bough!
In youth it sheltered me,
And I'll protect it now.
'T was my forefather's hand
  That placed it near his cot;
There, woodman, let it stand,
  Thy axe shall harm it not.

That old familiar tree,
Whose glory and renown
Are spread o'er land and sea—
And wouldst thou hew it down?
Woodman, forbear thy stroke!
  Cut not its earth-bound ties;
Oh, spare that aged oak
  Now towering to the skies ...

My heart-strings round thee cling,
  Close as thy bark, old friend!
Here shall the wild-bird sing,
  And still thy branches bend.
Old tree! the storm still brave!
  And, woodman, leave the spot;
While I've a hand to save,
  Thy axe shall harm it not.

GEORGE POPE MORRIS (1802-1864)

58 *from Afterwards*

WHEN the Present has latched its postern behind my
    tremulous stay,
    And the May month flaps its glad green leaves like wings,
Delicate-filmed as new-spun silk, will the neighbours say,
    'He was a man who used to notice such things'?

If it be in the dusk when, like an eyelid's soundless blink,
    The dewfall-hawk comes crossing the shades to alight
Upon the wind-warped upland thorn, a gazer may think,
    'To him this must have been a familiar sight.'

If I pass during some nocturnal blackness, mothy and warm,
    When the hedgehog travels furtively over the lawn,
One may say, 'He strove that such innocent creatures should
    come to no harm,
    But he could do little for them; and now he is gone' …

And will any say when my bell of quittance is heard in
    the gloom,
    And a crossing breeze cuts a pause in its outrollings,
Till they rise again, as they were a new bell's boom,
    'He hears it not now, but used to notice such things'?

THOMAS HARDY (1840-1928)

59 *from Ode to the West Wind*

O WILD West Wind, thou breath of Autumn's being,
  Thou from whose unseen presence the leaves dead
Are driven like ghosts from an enchanter fleeing,

  Yellow, and black, and pale, and hectic red,
Pestilence-stricken multitudes! O thou
  Who chariotest to their dark wintry bed

The wingèd seeds, where they lie cold and low,
  Each like a corpse within its grave, until
Thine azure sister of the Spring shall blow

  Her clarion o'er the dreaming earth, and fill
(Driving sweet buds like flocks to feed in air)
  With living hues and odours plain and hill;

Wild Spirit, which art moving everywhere;
Destroyer and preserver; hear, O hear! ...

Drive my dead thoughts over the universe,
  Like wither'd leaves, to quicken a new birth;
And, by the incantation of this verse,

  Scatter, as from an unextinguish'd hearth
Ashes and sparks, my words among mankind!
  Be through my lips to unawaken'd earth

The trumpet of a prophecy! O Wind,
If Winter comes, can Spring be far behind?

PERCY BYSSHE SHELLEY (1792-1822)

60 *from To Autumn*

SEASON of mists and mellow fruitfulness!
  Close bosom-friend of the maturing sun;
Conspiring with him how to load and bless
  With fruit the vines that round the thatch-eaves run;
To bend with apples the moss'd cottage-trees,
  And fill all fruit with ripeness to the core;
        To swell the gourd, and plump the hazel shells
With a sweet kernel; to set budding more,
  And still more, later flowers for the bees,
  Until they think warm days will never cease,
        For Summer has o'er brimm'd their clammy cells ...

Where are the songs of Spring? Ay, where are they?
  Think not of them, thou hast thy music too,—
While barred clouds bloom the soft-dying day,
  And touch the stubble-plains with rosy hue;
Then in a wailful choir the small gnats mourn
  Among the river sallows, borne aloft
        Or sinking as the light wind lives or dies;
And full-grown lambs loud bleat from hilly bourn;
  Hedge-crickets sing; and now with treble soft
  The redbreast whistles from a garden-croft;
        And gathering swallows twitter in the skies.

JOHN KEATS (1795-1821)

61 *from As You Like It*

                    ALL the world's a stage,
And all the men and women merely players:
They have their exits and their entrances;
And one man in his time plays many parts,
His acts being seven ages. At first the infant,
Mewling and puking in the nurse's arms.
And then the whining schoolboy, with his satchel,
And shining morning face, creeping like snail
Unwillingly to school. And then the lover,
Sighing like furnace, with a woeful ballad
Made to his mistress' eyebrow. Then a soldier,
Full of strange oaths, and bearded like the pard.
                    … And then the justice,
In fair round belly with good capon lined,
With eyes severe, and beard of formal cut,
Full of wise saws and modern instances;
And so he plays his part. The sixth age shifts
Into the lean and slippered pantaloon
With spectacles on nose and pouch on side;
His youthful hose, well saved, a world too wide
For his shrunk shank, and his big manly voice,
Turning again towards childish treble, pipes
And whistles in his sound. Last scene of all,
That ends this strange eventful history,
Is second childishness and mere oblivion,
Sans teeth, sans eyes, sans taste, sans everything.

WILLIAM SHAKESPEARE (1564-1616)

62 *from Elegy Written in a Country Churchyard*

THE curfew tolls the knell of parting day,
  The lowing herd wind slowly o'er the lea,
The ploughman homeward plods his weary way,
  And leaves the world to darkness and to me.

Now fades the glimmering landscape on the sight,
  And all the air a solemn stillness holds,
Save where the beetle wheels his droning flight,
  And drowsy tinklings lull the distant folds;

Save that from yonder ivy-mantled tower
  The moping owl does to the moon complain
Of such, as wandering near her secret bower,
  Molest her ancient solitary reign.

Beneath those rugged elms, that yew-tree's shade,
  Where heaves the turf in many a mouldering heap,
Each in his narrow cell forever laid,
  The rude forefathers of the hamlet sleep …

THOMAS GRAY (1716-1771)

63 *For Whom the Bell Tolls, from Meditation 17*

NO MAN is an island, entire of itself; every man is a piece of the continent, a part of the main; if a clod be washed away by the sea, Europe is the less, as well as if a promontory were, as well as if a manor of thy friend's or of thine own were. Any man's death diminishes me, because I am involved in mankind; and therefore never send to know for whom the bells tolls; it tolls for thee.

JOHN DONNE (1572-1631)

64 *Do not go gentle into that good night*

DO NOT go gentle into that good night,
Old age should burn and rave at close of day;
Rage, rage against the dying of the light.

Though wise men at their end know dark is right,
Because their words had forked no lightning they
Do not go gentle into that good night.

Good men, the last wave by, crying how bright
Their frail deeds might have danced in a green bay,
Rage, rage against the dying of the light.

Wild men who caught and sang the sun in flight,
And learn, too late, they grieved it on its way,
Do not go gentle into that good night.

Grave men, near death, who see with blinding sight
Blind eyes could blaze like meteors and be gay,
Rage, rage against the dying of the light.

And you, my father, there on the sad height,
Curse, bless, me now with your fierce tears, I pray.
Do not go gentle into that good night.
Rage, rage against the dying of the light.

DYLAN THOMAS (1914-1953)

65 *Heraclitus*

THEY told me, Heraclitus, they told me you were dead,
They brought me bitter news to hear and bitter tears to shed.
I wept as I remembered how often you and I
Had tired the sun with talking and sent him down the sky.

And now that thou art lying, my dear old Carian guest,
A handful of grey ashes, long, long ago at rest,
Still are thy pleasant voices, thy nightingales, awake;
For Death, he taketh all away, but them he cannot take.

WILLIAM CORY (1823-1892)

66 *Funeral Blues*

STOP all the clocks, cut off the telephone,
Prevent the dog from barking with a juicy bone,
Silence the pianos and with muffled drum
Bring out the coffin, let the mourners come.

Let aeroplanes circle moaning overhead
Scribbling on the sky the message He Is Dead,
Put crêpe bows round the white necks of the public doves,
Let the traffic policemen wear black cotton gloves.

He was my North, my South, my East and West,
My working week and my Sunday rest,
My noon, my midnight, my talk, my song;
I thought that love would last for ever: I was wrong.

The stars are not wanted now: put out every one;
Pack up the moon and dismantle the sun;
Pour away the ocean and sweep up the wood.
For nothing now can ever come to any good.

W H AUDEN (1907-1973)

67 *Remember*

REMEMBER me when I am gone away,
   Gone far away into the silent land;
   When you can no more hold me by the hand,
Nor I half turn to go yet turning stay.
Remember me when no more day by day
   You tell me of our future that you planned:
   Only remember me; you understand
It will be late to counsel then or pray.
Yet if you should forget me for a while
   And afterwards remember, do not grieve:
   For if the darkness and corruption leave
   A vestige of the thoughts that once I had,
Better by far you should forget and smile
   Than that you should remember and be sad.

CHRISTINA ROSSETTI (1830-1894)

68 *The Old Familiar Faces*

I HAVE had playmates, I have had companions,
In my days of childhood, in my joyful school-days,
    All, all are gone, the old familiar faces.

I have been laughing, I have been carousing,
Drinking late, sitting late, with my bosom cronies,
    All, all are gone, the old familiar faces.

I loved a love once, fairest among women:
Closed are her doors on me, I must not see her—
    All, all are gone, the old familiar faces.

I have a friend, a kinder friend has no man;
Like an ingrate, I left my friend abruptly;
    Left him, to muse on the old familiar faces.

Ghost-like I paced round the haunts of my childhood,
Earth seemed a desert I was bound to traverse,
    Seeking to find the old familiar faces.

Friend of my bosom, thou more than a brother,
Why wert not thou born in my father's dwelling?
    So might we talk of the old familiar faces—

How some they have died, and some they have left me,
And some are taken from me; all are departed;
    All, all are gone, the old familiar faces.

CHARLES LAMB (1775-1834)

69 *Ozymandias*

I MET a traveller from an antique land
   Who said: Two vast and trunkless legs of stone
Stand in the desert ... Near them, on the sand,
   Half sunk, a shattered visage lies, whose frown,
And wrinkled lip, and sneer of cold command,
   Tell that its sculptor well those passions read
Which yet survive, stamped on these lifeless things,
   The hand that mocked them, and the heart that fed:

   And on the pedestal these words appear:
'My name is Ozymandias, king of kings:
   Look on my works, ye Mighty, and despair!'
Nothing beside remains. Round the decay
   Of that colossal wreck, boundless and bare
The lone and level sands stretch far away.

PERCY BYSSHE SHELLEY (1792-1822)

70 *The Nile*

IT FLOWS through old hushed Egypt and its sands,
Like some grave mighty thought threading a dream,
And times and things, as in that vision, seem
Keeping along it their eternal stands,—
Caves, pillars, pyramids, the shepherd bands
That roamed through the young world, the glory extreme
Of high Sesostris, and that southern beam,
The laughing queen that caught the world's great hands.
Then comes a mightier silence, stern and strong,
As of a world left empty of its throng,
And the void weighs on us; and then we wake,
And hear the fruitful stream lapsing along
'Twixt villages, and think how we shall take
Our own calm journey on for human sake.

LEIGH HUNT (1784-1859)

71 *Symphony in Yellow*

AN OMNIBUS across the bridge
  Crawls like a yellow butterfly,
  And, here and there, a passer-by
Shows like a little restless midge.
Big barges full of yellow hay
  Are moored against the shadowy wharf,
  And, like a yellow silken scarf,
The thick fog hangs along the quay.
The yellow leaves begin to fade
  And flutter from the Temple elms,
  And at my feet the pale green Thames
Lies like a rod of rippled jade.

OSCAR WILDE (1854-1900)

72 Adlestrop

YES, I remember Adlestrop—
The name, because one afternoon
Of heat the express-train drew up there
Unwontedly. It was late June.

The steam hissed. Someone cleared his throat.
No one left and no one came
On the bare platform. What I saw
Was Adlestrop—only the name

And willows, willow-herb, and grass,
And meadowsweet, and haycocks dry,
No whit less still and lonely fair
Than the high cloudlets in the sky.

And for that minute a blackbird sang
Close by, and round him, mistier,
Farther and farther, all the birds
Of Oxfordshire and Gloucestershire.

EDWARD THOMAS (1878-1917)

73 *From a Railway Carriage*

FASTER than fairies, faster than witches,
Bridges and houses, hedges and ditches,
And charging along like troops in a battle,
All through the meadows the horses and cattle
All of the sights of the hill and the plain
Fly as thick as driving rain;
And ever again, in the wink of an eye,
Painted stations whistle by.
Here is a child who clambers and scrambles,
All by himself and gathering brambles;
Here is a tramp who stands and gazes;
And there is the green for stringing the daisies!
Here is a cart run away in the road
Lumping along with man and load;
And here is a mill, and there is a river
Each a glimpse and gone forever!

ROBERT LOUIS STEVENSON (1850-1894)

74 *Travel*

THE railroad track is miles away,
And the day is loud with voices speaking,
Yet there isn't a train goes by all day
But I hear its whistle shrieking.
All night there isn't a train goes by,
Though the night is still for sleep and dreaming,
But I see its cinders red on the sky,
And hear its engine steaming.
My heart is warm with friends I make,
And better friends I not be knowing;
Yet there isn't a train I'd rather take,
No matter where it's going.

EDNA ST VINCENT MILLAY (1892-1950)

75 *from Night Mail*

THIS is the Night Mail crossing the border,
Bringing the cheque and the postal order,
Letters for the rich, letters for the poor,
The shop at the corner, the girl next door.
Pulling up Beattock, a steady climb:
The gradient's against her, but she's on time.
Past cotton-grass and moorland boulder,
Shovelling white steam over her shoulder,
Snorting noisily, she passes
Silent miles of wind-bent grasses.
Birds turn their heads as she approaches,
Stare from the bushes at her blank-faced coaches.
Sheep-dogs cannot turn her course;
They slumber on with paws across.
In the farm she passes no one wakes,
But a jug in a bedroom gently shakes ...

W H AUDEN (1907-1973)

76 *Home Thoughts from Abroad*

OH, TO be in England
Now that April's there,
And whoever wakes in England
Sees, some morning, unaware,
That the lowest boughs and the brushwood sheaf
Round the elm-tree bole are in tiny leaf,
While the chaffinch sings on the orchard bough
In England—now!

And after April, when May follows,
And the whitethroat builds, and all the swallows!
Hark, where my blossomed pear-tree in the hedge
Leans to the field and scatters on the clover
Blossoms and dewdrops—at the bent spray's edge—
That's the wise thrush; he sings each song twice over,
Lest you should think he never could recapture
The first fine careless rapture!
And though the fields look rough with hoary dew,
All will be gay when noontide wakes anew
The buttercups, the little children's dower
—Far brighter than this gaudy melon-flower!

ROBERT BROWNING (1812-1889)

77 from The Old Vicarage, Grantchester

... Ah God! to see the branches stir
Across the moon at Grantchester!
To smell the thrilling-sweet and rotten
Unforgettable, unforgotten
River-smell, and hear the breeze
Sobbing in the little trees.
Say, do the elm-clumps greatly stand
Still guardians of that holy land?
The chestnuts shade, in reverend dream,
The yet unacademic stream?
Is dawn a secret shy and cold
Anadyomene, silver-gold?
And sunset still a golden sea
From Haslingfield to Madingley?
And after, ere the night is born,
Do hares come out about the corn?
Oh, is the water sweet and cool,
Gentle and brown, above the pool?
And laughs the immortal river still
Under the mill, under the mill?
Say, is there Beauty yet to find?
And Certainty? and Quiet kind?
Deep meadows yet, for to forget
The lies, and truths, and pain? ... oh! yet
Stands the Church clock at ten to three?
And is there honey still for tea?

RUPERT BROOKE (1887-1915)

78 *maggie and milly and molly and may*

maggie and milly and molly and may
went down to the beach(to play one day)

and maggie discovered a shell that sang
so sweetly she couldn't remember her troubles,and

milly befriended a stranded star
whose rays five languid fingers were;

and molly was chased by a horrible thing
which raced sideways while blowing bubbles:and

may came home with a smooth round stone
as small as a world and as large as alone.

For whatever we lose(like a you or a me)
it's always ourselves we find in the sea

E E CUMMINGS (1894-1962)

79 *from Jabberwocky*

'TWAS brillig, and the slithy toves
    Did gyre and gimble in the wabe;
All mimsy were the borogoves,
    And the mome raths outgrabe.

'Beware the Jabberwock, my son!
    The jaws that bite, the claws that catch!
Beware the Jubjub bird, and shun
    The frumious Bandersnatch!'

He took his vorpal sword in hand:
    Long time the manxome foe he sought—
So rested he by the Tumtum tree,
    And stood awhile in thought.

And, as in uffish thought he stood,
    The Jabberwock, with eyes of flame,
Came whiffling through the tulgy wood,
    And burbled as it came!

One two! One two! And through and through
    The vorpal blade went snicker-snack!
He left it dead, and with its head
    He went galumphing back.

'And hast thou slain the Jabberwock?
    Come to my arms, my beamish boy!
O frabjous day! Callooh! Callay!'
    He chortled in his joy …

LEWIS CARROLL (1832-1898)

80 *from The Fairies*

UP THE airy mountain
Down the rushy glen,
We daren't go a-hunting,
For fear of little men;
Wee folk, good folk,
Trooping all together;
Green jacket, red cap,
And white owl's feather.
Down along the rocky shore
Some make their home,
They live on crispy pancakes
Of yellow tide-foam;
Some in the reeds
Of the black mountain-lake,
With frogs for their watch-dogs,
All night awake …

WILLIAM ALLINGHAM (1824-1889)

81 *from The Owl and the Pussy-cat*

THE Owl and the Pussy-cat went to sea
   In a beautiful pea-green boat,
They took some honey, and plenty of money,
   Wrapped up in a five-pound note.
The Owl looked up to the stars above,
   And sang to a small guitar,
'O lovely Pussy! O Pussy, my love,
     What a beautiful Pussy you are,
       You are,
       You are!
   What a beautiful Pussy you are' …

'Dear Pig, are you willing to sell for one shilling
   Your ring?' Said the Piggy, 'I will.'
So they took it away, and were married next day
   By the Turkey who lives on the hill.
They dined on mince, and slices of quince,
   Which they ate with a runcible spoon;
And hand in hand, on the edge of the sand,
     They danced by the light of the moon,
       The moon,
       The moon,
   They danced by the light of the moon.

EDWARD LEAR (1812-1888)

82 *from The Walrus and the Carpenter*

... 'O OYSTERS, come and walk with us!'
The Walrus did beseech.
'A pleasant walk, a pleasant talk,
Along the briny beach:
We cannot do with more than four,
To give a hand to each' ...

The Walrus and the Carpenter
Walked on a mile or so,
And then they rested on a rock
Conveniently low:
And all the little Oysters stood
And waited in a row.

'The time has come,' the Walrus said,
'To talk of many things:
Of shoes—and ships—and sealing-wax—
Of cabbages—and kings—
And why the sea is boiling hot—
And whether pigs have wings' ...

LEWIS CARROLL (1832-1898)

83 *from The Pirates of Penzance*

I AM the very model of a modern Major-General,
    I've information vegetable, animal, and mineral,
    I know the kings of England, and I quote the fights
        historical
    From Marathon to Waterloo, in order categorical;
    I'm very well acquainted, too, with matters
        mathematical,
    I understand equations, both the simple and
        quadratical,
    About binomial theorem I'm teeming with a lot o' news,
    With many cheerful facts about the square of the
        hypotenuse …

W S GILBERT (1836-1911)

84 *from You are old, Father William...*

'YOU are old, Father William,' the young man said,
'And your hair has become very white;
And yet you incessantly stand on your head—
Do you think, at your age, it is right?'
'In my youth,' Father William replied to his son,
'I feared it might injure the brain;
But now that I'm perfectly sure I have none,
Why, I do it again and again' ...

LEWIS CARROLL (1832-1898)

85 *from Children's Hour*

BETWEEN the dark and the daylight,
When the night is beginning to lower,
Comes a pause in the day's occupations,
That is known as the Children's Hour.
I hear in the chamber above me
The patter of little feet,
The sound of a door that is opened,
And voices soft and sweet.
From my study I see in the lamplight,
Descending the broad hall stair,
Grave Alice, and laughing Allegra,
And Edith with golden hair.
They whisper, and then a silence;
Yet I know by their merry eyes
They are plotting and planning together
To take me by surprise.
A sudden rush from the stairway,
A sudden raid from the hall!
By three doors left unguarded
They enter my castle wall!
They climb up into my turret
O'er the arms and back of my chair;
If I try to escape, they surround me;
They seem to be everywhere …

HENRY WADSWORTH LONGFELLOW (1807-1882)

86 *from The Mikado*

THREE little maids from school are we
Pert as a school-girl well can be
Filled to the brim with girlish glee
Three little maids from school

Everything is a source of fun
Nobody's safe, for we care for none
Life is a joke that's just begun
Three little maids from school

Three little maids who, all unwary
Come from a ladies' seminary
Freed from its genius tutelary
Three little maids from school
Three little maids from school ...

W S GILBERT (1836-1911)

87 *from Kubla Khan*

IN XANADU did Kubla Khan
A stately pleasure-dome decree:
Where Alph, the sacred river, ran
Through caverns measureless to man
    Down to a sunless sea.
So twice five miles of fertile ground
With walls and towers were girdled round:
And there were gardens bright with sinuous rills,
Where blossomed many an incense-bearing tree;
And here were forests ancient as the hills,
Enfolding sunny spots of greenery.

But oh! that deep romantic chasm which slanted
Down the green hill athwart a cedarn cover!
A savage place! as holy and enchanted
As e'er beneath a waning moon was haunted
By woman wailing for her demon-lover!
And from this chasm, with ceaseless turmoil seething,
As if this earth in fast thick pants were breathing,
A mighty fountain momently was forced:
Amid whose swift half-intermitted burst
Huge fragments vaulted like rebounding hail,
Or chaffy grain beneath the thresher's flail:
And 'mid these dancing rocks at once and ever
It flung up momently the sacred river …

SAMUEL TAYLOR COLERIDGE (1772-1834)

88 *The Donkey*

WHEN fishes flew and forests walked
   And figs grew upon thorn,
Some moment when the moon was blood
   Then surely I was born.

With monstrous head and sickening cry
   And ears like errant wings,
The devil's walking parody
   On all four-footed things.

The tattered outlaw of the earth,
   Of ancient crooked will;
Starve, scourge, deride me: I am dumb,
   I keep my secret still.

Fools! For I also had my hour;
   One far fierce hour and sweet:
There was a shout about my ears,
   And palms before my feet.

G K CHESTERTON (1874-1936)

89 *from The Tyger*

TYGER! Tyger! burning bright
In the forests of the night
What immortal hand or eye
Could frame thy fearful symmetry?

In what distant deeps or skies
Burnt the fire of thine eyes?
On what wings dare he aspire?
What the hand dare sieze the fire?

And what shoulder, & what art,
Could twist the sinews of thy heart?
And when thy heart began to beat,
What dread hand? & what dread feet? ...

When the stars threw down their spears,
And watered heaven with their tears,
Did he smile his work to see?
Did he who made the Lamb make thee?

Tyger! Tyger! burning bright
In the forests of the night,
What immortal hand or eye
Dare frame thy fearful symmetry.

WILLIAM BLAKE (1757-1827)

90 *The More Loving One*

LOOKING up at the stars, I know quite well
That, for all they care, I can go to hell,
But on earth indifference is the least
We have to dread from man or beast.

How should we like it were stars to burn
With a passion for us we could not return?
If equal affection cannot be,
Let the more loving one be me.

Admirer as I think I am
Of stars that do not give a damn,
I cannot, now I see them, say
I missed one terribly all day.

Were all stars to disappear or die,
I should learn to look at an empty sky
And feel its total dark sublime,
Though this might take me a little time.

W H AUDEN (1907-1973)

91 *from Light Shining Out of Darkness*

GOD moves in a mysterious way,
    His wonders to perform;
He plants his footsteps in the sea,
    And rides upon the storm.

Deep in unfathomable mines
    Of never failing skill
He treasures up his bright designs,
    And works his sovereign will ...

Judge not the Lord by feeble sense,
    But trust him for His grace;
Behind a frowning providence
    He hides a smiling face.

His purposes will ripen fast,
    Unfolding every hour;
The bud may have a bitter taste,
    But sweet will be the flower.

Blind unbelief is sure to err,
    And scan his work in vain;
God is his own interpreter,
    And he will make it plain.

WILLIAM COWPER (1731-1800)

92 *Les Ballons*

AGAINST these turbid turquoise skies
The light and luminous balloons
Dip and drift like satin moons
Drift like silken butterflies;
Reel with every windy gust,
Rise and reel like dancing girls,
Float like strange transparent pearls,
Fall and float like silver dust.
Now to the low leaves they cling,
Each with coy fantastic pose,
Each a petal of a rose
Straining at a gossamer string.
Then to the tall trees they climb,
Like thin globes of amethyst,
Wandering opals keeping tryst
With the rubies of the lime.

OSCAR WILDE (1854-1900)

93 *The Rainbow*

MY HEART leaps up when I behold
      A rainbow in the sky:
So was it when my life began;
So is it now I am a man;
So be it when I shall grow old,
      Or let me die!
The Child is father of the Man;
And I could wish my days to be
Bound each to each by natural piety.

WILLIAM WORDSWORTH (1770-1850)

94 *from An Essay on Man*

KNOW then thyself, presume not God to scan;
The proper study of mankind is Man.
Placed on this isthmus of a middle state,
A being darkly wise, and rudely great:
With too much knowledge for the Sceptic side,
With too much weakness for the Stoic's pride,
He hangs between; in doubt to act or rest,
In doubt to deem himself a God or Beast,
In doubt his mind or body to prefer;
Born but to die, and reasoning but to err;
Alike in ignorance, his reason such
Whether he thinks too little or too much:
Chaos of thought and passion, all confused;
Still by himself abused, or disabused;
Created half to rise and half to fall;
Great lord of all things, yet a prey to all;
Sole judge of truth, in endless error hurled:
The glory, jest, and riddle of the world! ...

ALEXANDER POPE (1688-1744)

95 *from Intimations of Immortality*

... OUR birth is but a sleep and a forgetting:
  The Soul that rises with us, our life's Star,
          Hath had elsewhere its setting,
              And cometh from afar:
            Not in entire forgetfulness,
            And not in utter nakedness,
  But trailing clouds of glory do we come
          From God, who is our home:
  Heaven lies about us in our infancy!
  Shades of the prison-house begin to close
            Upon the growing Boy,
  But he beholds the light, and whence it flows,
          He sees it in his joy;
  The Youth, who daily farther from the east
          Must travel, still is Nature's priest,
            And by the vision splendid
              Is on his way attended;
  At length the Man perceives it die away,
  And fade into the light of common day ...

WILLIAM WORDSWORTH (1770-1850)

96 *from The Princess*

THE splendour falls on castle walls
    And snowy summits old in story:
The long light shakes across the lakes,
    And the wild cataract leaps in glory.
Blow, bugle, blow, set the wild echoes flying,
Blow, bugle; answer, echoes, dying, dying, dying.

O hark, O hear! how thin and clear,
    And thinner, clearer, farther going!
O sweet and far from cliff and scar
    The horns of Elfland faintly blowing!
Blow, let us hear the purple glens replying:
Blow, bugle; answer, echoes, dying, dying, dying.

O love, they die in yon rich sky,
    They faint on hill or field or river:
Our echoes roll from soul to soul,
    And grow forever and forever.
Blow, bugle, blow, set the wild echoes flying,
And answer, echoes, answer, dying, dying, dying.

ALFRED, LORD TENNYSON (1809-1892)

97 Music, When Soft Voices Die

MUSIC, when soft voices die,
Vibrates in the memory—
Odours, when sweet violets sicken,
Live within the sense they quicken.

Rose leaves, when the rose is dead,
Are heaped for the beloved's bed;
And so thy thoughts, when thou art
   gone,
Love itself shall slumber on.

PERCY BYSSHE SHELLEY (1792-1822)

98 *Everyone Sang*

EVERYONE suddenly burst out singing;
And I was filled with such delight
As prisoned birds must find in freedom,
Winging wildly across the white
Orchards and dark-green fields; on—on—and
    out of sight.

Everyone's voice was suddenly lifted;
And beauty came like the setting sun:
My heart was shaken with tears; and horror
Drifted away … O, but Everyone
Was a bird; and the song was wordless; the singing
    will never be done.

SIEGFRIED SASSOON (1886-1967)

99 *Jerusalem, from Milton*

AND did those feet in ancient time
Walk upon England's mountains green?
And was the holy Lamb of God
On England's pleasant pastures seen?

And did the Countenance Divine
Shine forth upon our clouded hills?
And was Jerusalem builded here
Among these dark Satanic Mills?

Bring me my Bow of burning gold:
Bring me my Arrows of desire:
Bring me my Spear: O clouds unfold!
Bring me my Chariot of fire.

I will not cease from Mental Fight,
Nor shall my Sword sleep in my hand
Till we have built Jerusalem
In England's green & pleasant Land.

WILLIAM BLAKE (1757-1827)

100 *from The Passionate Man's Pilgrimage*

GIVE me my scallop-shell of quiet,
My staff of faith to walk upon,
My scrip of joy, immortal diet,
My bottle of salvation,
My gown of glory, hope's true gage,
And thus I'll take my pilgrimage.

Blood must be my body's balmer,
No other balm will there be given,
Whilst my soul, like a white palmer,
Travels to the land of heaven;
Over the silver mountains,
Where spring the nectar fountains;
And there I'll kiss
The bowl of bliss,
And drink my eternal fill
On every milken hill.
My soul will be a-dry before,
But after it will ne'er thirst more …

SIR WALTER RALEIGH (?1552-1618)

FIRST LINE INDEX

ACKNOWLEDGEMENTS

The publishers would like to acknowledge the following for permission to reproduce copyright poems in this collection.

W H Auden, 'Funeral Blues', 'Night Mail' and 'The More Loving One' from Collected Poems. Reprinted with the permission of Faber & Faber.

John Betjeman, 'East Anglian Bathe' from Collected Poems. Reprinted with the permission of John Murray (Publishers) Ltd.

G K Chesterton, 'The Donkey' from Modern British Poetry, Untermeyer, Louis (ed). New York, Harcourt, Brace and Howe, 1920. Reprinted with the permission of A P Watt Ltd on behalf of the Royal Literary Fund.

Frances Cornford, 'Childhood' from Collected Poems, published by Cresset Press. Reprinted with the permission of The Random House Group Ltd.

E E Cummings, 'maggie and milly and molly and may' is reprinted from Complete Poems 1904-1962, by E. E. Cummings, edited by George J. Firmage, by permission of W. W. Norton & Company. Copyright ©1991 by the Trustees for the E. E. Cummings Trust and George James Firmage.

W H Davies, "Leisure' reproduced with the permission of Dee & Griffin, on behalf of the Mrs H M Davies Will Trust.

Robert Frost, 'The Road Not Taken' from The Poetry of Robert Frost edited by Edward Connery Lathem, published by Jonathan Cape. Reprinted with the permission of The Random House Group Ltd.

Rudyard Kipling, 'If' from Rudyard Kipling's Verse: Definitive Edition. Reprinted with the permission of A P Watt Ltd., on behalf of The National Trust for Places of Historic Interest or Natural Beauty.

D H Lawrence, 'Baby Tortoise', 'The Elephant is Slow To Mate', The Collected Poems of D H Lawrence (Penguin, London, 1994). By kind permission of Laurence Pollinger Limited and the Estate of Frieda Lawrence Ravagli.

Edna St Vincent Millay, 'Travel' and 'Afternoon on a Hill' from Collected Poems (New York: HarperCollins Publishers, 1982). Reprinted with the permission of Elizabeth Barnett, Literary Executor.

Sylvia Plath, 'Child' and 'Morning Song" from Collected Poems. Reprinted with the permission of Faber & Faber.

Siegfried Sassoon, "Everyone Sang', copyright Siegfried Sassoon by kind permission of George Sassoon.

Dylan Thomas, 'Do Not Go Gentle Into That Good Night', Dylan Thomas, Collected Poems, J. M. Dent (ed.). Reprinted with permission of David Higham Associates.

W B Yeats, 'The Lake Isle of Innisfree' from The Poems of W B Yeats: A New Edition, edited by R J Finneran. Copyright ©1940 by Georgie Yeats, renewed 1968 by Bertha Georgie Yeats. Reprinted with the permission of A P Watt Ltd., on behalf of Michael Yeats.

Although the publishers have tried to contact all copyright holders before publication, this has not proved possible in every case. If notified, the publisher will be pleased to make any necessary arrangements.